GREAT MASTERPIECES BY

Van Gogh

GREAT MASTERPIECES BY

Van Gogh

Introduction and Commentaries by

J. PATRICE MARANDEL

Curator, Museum of Fine Arts, Houston

AN **Artabras** BOOK

CROWN PUBLISHERS, INC. • NEW YORK, N.Y.

O<small>N THE</small> F<small>RONT</small> C<small>OVER</small>
  Self-Portrait with Bandaged Ear

O<small>N THE</small> T<small>ITLE</small> P<small>AGE</small>
  Flowering Almond Branch

O<small>N THE</small> B<small>ACK</small> C<small>OVER</small>
  Van Gogh's Bedroom at Arles

Commentaries on page 104

All quotations from *The Complete Letters of Vincent van Gogh,* published by the New York Graphic Society, Copyright © 1966

The Publisher wishes to thank the New York Graphic Society and Little Brown & Co. for their permission to quote.

Library of Congress Catalog Card Number: 79-55262

ISBN: 0-517-28750-1

CONTENTS

INTRODUCTION

Can the life of an artist explain his work? A commonly held view tends to make the struggles of any committed artist a component of his personality, and even of his style. Yet to take examples from among van Gogh's contemporaries only, the incomprehension Monet or Renoir had to face at the beginning of their careers never reflected upon the quality of their work any more than the uneventful life of Seurat can account for the extraordinary impact of his production or its quiet appearance. The case is different with van Gogh. Never did an artist identify himself so closely with his work. So closely interwoven are his life and art that his paintings do not merely "reflect" his sufferings: they *are* his anguish, his fears, and occasionally, his joy.

Van Gogh's life can be read superficially, like any account of the progression of a painter of his time: years in college, apprenticeship—not with an artist but in the firm of an art dealer—the decision to become a painter, a wandering between several places with the obligatory stay in Paris, friendships and encounters with other artists, and finally the development of a personal style. In the course of his life, even his illness and suicide become part of a scheme that could be common to many other artists. What makes his life so different from others is its intensity. Each period of his career, marked by a move from one place to another, has its passion, as if he had thoroughly exhausted the possibilities of the situation. Each one ends in a personal or intellectual crisis: the break with Holland, with a slow maturation that led him to accept himself as a painter; the search for light in the South and his hope to establish a colony of artists there; self-mutilation and an internment in a hospital until its unsufferability prompted his release; and ultimately, his suicide. Much has been said about van Gogh's insanity. It has given many the opportunity to apply medical or psychological theories to the deciphering of his work, but the nature of his illness remains obscure: epileptic, schizophrenic? His mental illness was part of his life—something van Gogh painfully learned to live with. It does not account for the way he painted, or for what he painted; and even less does it account for his genius. Before being a madman, van Gogh was, above all, a great artist.

Vincent van Gogh was born on March 30, 1853, at Groot-Zundert, the son of a pastor. His childhood was spent in a stern village, under a gray sky. For generations the men in his family had been ministers or art dealers. This dual heritage awakened at an early age his visual sense and instilled in him a profound respect for human values, for earnest and hard work—qualities associated with the puritanical tradition. After some unsuccessful attempts at becoming an art dealer—an apprenticeship that took him to the Hague, London, and Paris, and gave him a chance to acquaint himself with the works of the Hague school painters, Anton Mauve in particular, and the Barbizon

painters in France—van Gogh decided to turn to the other family tradition and to become a pastor. For two years, from 1878 until 1880, he tried honestly to embrace this profession, but he failed at it. This period of his life, notably the years spent among poor workers in the coal mining district of Belgium called the Borinage, remained throughout his life a constant reminder of human suffering. He witnessed human labor and misery and later equated his own sufferings with those of the miners. His profound sympathy for this world did not turn—strangely, perhaps, for this contemporary of Karl Marx—into socialist fervor but was instead sublimated into mystical glorification. His life among the poor and fallen humanity—he subsequently lived in the Hague with a drunken prostitute in complete squalor—has a Dostoievskian overtone. Like Dostoievski's heroes, he found among these people biblical values. The peasants of Nuenen—a city to which he moved shortly afterwards—belonged to the same social class. Poor, hard-working, their hands and faces betrayed time and labor. There he executed his first ambitious painting, *The Potato Eaters,* a work that in spite of its clumsiness—or because of it—adheres strictly to the code of ethics he was developing. He saw himself not only as a painter of peasants, but as a peasant painter, a worker whose production should take part in the cycle of the seasons or the growth of nature and ought to be regulated by it. He wanted to do honest work and for that reason did not seek a refined palette; instead, he painted in a rough and brutal manner, which befitted his subject. Portraits obsessed him because in a face he would see the expression of nature more than in a landscape. If he painted a landscape, however, he did it in the same direct way. A few years later, at Arles, he continued to paint landscapes and people with equal passion.

In 1886 van Gogh decided to move from the North to Paris, and the break was tremendous. His main reason for moving was to be closer to his brother Théo, who alone could soothe him and give direction to his life. He arrived there an almost untrained and unskilled painter, but in four years, until his death in 1890, he developed a personal style and a tremendous body of work, which was to change the course of art. 1886 turned out to be an important year for many painters: the last impressionist exhibition and Seurat's exhibition of his *Grande-Jatte* took place that year. In the aftermath of the impressionist upheaval, van Gogh responded to the message of these painters: his subject matter became disengaged, his palette lighter, and he adopted a finer and divided brushstroke. Very much his own man, he never adhered strictly to a principle, and he gathered from various painters whatever served his own purpose. He admired Seurat for the simplicity of his style and saw the extraordinary possibilities opened by his pointillist technique; but he never adopted it rigorously. As for the impressionists, their work quickly became too refined and too "urban" for van Gogh, who preferred to it the expressiveness reintroduced by younger artists, such as Toulouse-Lautrec or Gauguin. The blurred image of the impressionists was also opposed to van Gogh's new discovery: Japonism (although the impressionists had explored their own relationship to Japonism, using, above all, compositional devices borrowed from Japanese prints). For van Gogh, Japan was a "world of pure colors," and he was attracted in these exotic works to the almost barbaric juxtaposition—by European standards—of flat colors and the neatly outlined drawing of the figures, which enhanced their expressiveness. He immediately saw how to transform this purely formal language into a highly expressive one, achieved by the preponderant role he gave to color. He moved from the literal use of colors, which had been characteristic of his Nuenen period, to the elaboration of a highly sophisticated grammar of colors in which each one is associated with a mood or the expression of a feeling. Especially after his move to Arles in 1888, colors have their own life and replace an abundance of details. Yellow, the color of the sun, expresses in its infinite gradations various joyful and celebrating moods. Blue—a more muted color of the sky and of the night—expresses a deep intensity of feeling. Van Gogh displayed these colors behind the sitters for his portraits, like banners clearly announcing the emotional intensity of the work.

Arles was van Gogh's Japan. Under the sun, he could see colors he had never experienced before. Seen in the total context of his oeuvre, the production of the eighteen months he spent there appears as the central—and crucial—panel of a polypitch framed by Nuenen and Paris on one side, Saint-Rémy and Auvers on the other. Both in individual works and as a whole, the Arles production presents a remarkable coherence. The same spirit pervades portraits, landscapes, and still lifes alike: the light of the South shines over a sunny field, illuminates a portrait, and glows even in the darkest night. Plenitude is expressed through a "masculine" control of the brush. The mannerisms of Paris have been forgotten, the clumsiness of Nuenen magically transformed into a robust and immediate style. His fascination for the South intoxicated him, and his missionary attitude prompted him to invite other artists. He elaborated the project of a colony centered around his newly decorated house. When Gauguin finally yielded to his plea and came south, illusions and expectations crumbled. The harmonious plan did not survive the clash of opposite personalities. On Christmas Eve, 1889, after a fight with Gauguin, van Gogh cut off his ear, and Gauguin left in the night for Paris. Théo came to Arles for a few days, but the dream had ended: van Gogh had suffered his first death.

A few weeks later, van Gogh entered the mental institution at nearby Saint-Rémy. In order to improve his mental state, he had voluntarily relinquished his freedom and left behind him the few friends he had made in Arles. He quickly realized that his confinement was suffocating. He accepted it with resignation, however, but his work changed eloquently. Deprived of sitters, he turned to memories and either painted people he had known at Arles or executed copies after prints he liked. He painted landscapes from his window or on occasional outings under hospital surveillance. These do not have the joyful openness of his Arles landscapes; they are closed-in compositions, intricate and almost devoid of sky. Colors are somewhat muted and affect a "Parisian" grayness. The drawing is dizzying and convulsive, elements and things participate in a swirling world, clouds and earth, trees and figures follow a like rhythm, which now replaces the color structure of the paintings done at Arles.

The insufferability of his condition and the fact that by medical standards he was considered improved prompted his release from Saint-Rémy. After a few days in Paris with Théo, who had married in the meantime and become a father—causing ambivalent reactions in van Gogh—he arrived in Auvers, a small town north of Paris, which had been visited by many impressionist painters as well as by Cézanne. He found in Dr. Gachet, to whom he had been recommended, a sympathetic character who could understand not only his illness but also his art; Gachet he was himself a collector of avantgarde paintings. Van Gogh thought of him as another self and painted his portrait in a style that shows compassion, understanding, and sadness. Although van Gogh was relatively happy at Auvers, he knew that his mental balance was still precarious. He managed, however, to paint with passion and executed in the weeks that preceded his death a large number of canvases. The landscapes curiously hark back to a somewhat earlier style. Although he maintains the powerful drawing he had elaborated in his paintings at Saint-Rémy, the colors are strong but lack the brilliance of the Mediterranean light. Once again in the light of the North, van Gogh was rediscovering his attachment to the earth. The houses, village streets, and churches he painted then are deeply rooted and writhing forms. Bound to the soil, they strive vehemently toward the sky. The sky itself affects a new appearance: it is not the plain, flawless sky of the South or the cosmic vision of the *Starry Night*. It is an intensely painted surface, charged with an emotion in which a presence is felt but rarely represented. In the *Church at Auvers,* a celestial body—moon or sun—belongs in color and texture to the sky.

A feeling of growth and a confusion of elements characterizes these last works. Men and stones, trees and clouds are made of the same substance. This visual pantheism is particularly evident in his spectacular *Wheatfield with Crows,* a painting that poignantly closes his work: earth and sky, background and foreground, and metaphorically, madness and reason are one in this painting. It was executed in the field where a few days later van Gogh shot himself to death. Its disquieting silence makes even more relevant the note he left in his pocket for Théo: "We can only make our pictures speak."

J. PATRICE MARANDEL

GREAT MASTERPIECES BY

Van Gogh

Girl in White Among Trees, 1882

Oil on canvas · 15⅜ × 23¼″ · Otterlo, Rijksmuseum Kröller-Müller

IN JANUARY, 1882, VAN GOGH ARRIVED IN THE HAGUE, hoping to gain admittance to the studio of one of the prominent local painters. Anton Mauve was the most respected of all, a serious academic painter who had achieved a considerable international reputation. Van Gogh admired him throughout his life and, at the time of Mauve's death, sent to a Dutch dealer a painting he had executed in Arles as an homage to him. While in his studio, however, he found the teaching unbearable, and after having broken a plaster cast, he left. Besides his struggle to become an artist, his personal life was unhappy: he was living with a drunken prostitute in complete squalor in an attachment that lasted for almost twenty months.

Van Gogh's early attempts at painting testify to his efforts to capture the essence of a Dutch tradition that he greatly admired and wanted to become part of. Yet an instinct for naturalism prevails in these early works. He worked hard on this small picture, inspired by an engraving by the British illustrator Perry McQuoid. It gave him confidence, however, that one day he could "make regularly something good every day." One is already struck by the ability of the aspiring artist to create a convincing space and to animate so brilliantly the surface of the painting. One notices also the distribution of colors, with little strokes responding to each other all over the canvas. Van Gogh wrote about "the great difficulty of keeping it clear, and of getting the space between the trunks standing at different distances —and the place and relative bulk of those trunks change with the perspective—to make it so one can breathe and walk around it, and to make you smell the fragrance of the wood."

The Potato Eaters, 1885

Oil on canvas · 32 × 44¾″ · Amsterdam, Rijksmuseum Vincent van Gogh

Bᴏᴛʜ ᴇsᴛʜᴇᴛɪᴄᴀʟʟʏ ᴀɴᴅ ᴘʜɪʟᴏsᴏᴘʜɪᴄᴀʟʟʏ, this picture sums up van Gogh's concerns during his stay at Nuenen. Many studies of individual heads, hands, cups, and other details, which reappear in the work, testify to van Gogh's application. Yet the finished composition is surprising in its clumsiness, its awkward rendition of space, and its unrefined handling of paint. The painter said of it: "It would be wrong . . . to give a peasant picture a . . . conventional smoothness."

In the brutal reality of the life of the peasants van Gogh found a counterpart to his own sufferings. He was poor, unrecognized by society, yet eager to share and to communicate, and these figures serve as metaphors for the painter himself. Van Gogh was not content, however, to translate as realistically as possible the life of his subjects, and the symbolic intention of the painting is evident. The honesty of the peasants' frugal life and their dedication to their humble work are qualities van Gogh admired and tried to translate in painterly terms. To indicate their intimate relationship to their work, he decided to color the faces of his figures in hues of "dusty potatoes." He was fond of saying at that time that Millet's peasants seemed to be made of the grains they were sowing.

Jean-François Millet was indeed the main influence on van Gogh during this period. Van Gogh made copies of Millet's works and, like him, succeeded in conferring on his most common scenes a deep religious feeling. Van Gogh's own rejection of an established religion led him to embrace a humanistic credo that finds its expression in this modern icon. Yet its composition betrays van Gogh's knowledge of more traditional religious representations. Echoes of Leonardo's *Last Supper*, of Dutch seventeenth-century painters (whom he admired for painting, as he did himself in this work, "black which has light in it"), and above all, of Caravaggesque paintings pervade the composition, not only in its formal arrangement of figures but also in its use of darker colors, of hidden sources of light (such as the one mysteriously emanating from the potato platter), and its insistence on the physical presence of objects.

Montmartre (The Terrace of the Moulin de la Galette), 1886

Oil on canvas · 17⅜ × 13⅛″ · The Art Institute of Chicago,
Helen Birch Bartlett Memorial Collection

SHORTLY AFTER ARRIVING IN PARIS, van Gogh executed this painting, one of many devoted to Montmartre (see *Moulin de la Galette*). An acute sense for a thin atmospheric quality—directly assimilated from the impressionists, to whom he had been only barely exposed—replaces advantageously a cumbersome accumulation of anecdotal details. Nothing actually indicates that the painting is of Paris: the view of the city is blurred in a sealike vastness, hardly distinct from the sky, and only the lampposts might give a clue to the urban nature of the scene. Yet the painting is typically Parisian in its rapid notations of light, people, and surroundings. Van Gogh adopts the almost perverse viewpoint of the impressionists, a slightly slanted but suggestive view, which is the opposite of the painstaking panoramas he had painted in the North.

With a freshness of execution usually reserved for watercolor, van Gogh carefully blends pale tones, a new element in his work. Subtle grays control the color scheme of the picture. Each tone accents or balances softly a shade of gray, but never overpowers it; for instance, the reddish twigs of the trees or the yellow post surprisingly divide the fence and save it from monotony. The improvised appearance of the picture is a quality peculiar to van Gogh. The drawing is free to the point of appearing nonexistent, yet the rhythmic coherence of the painting relies upon the geometric distribution of verticals—lamps, posts, and vine-trellis—while its delicacy results from the remarkable softness of the brushwork.

Moulin de la Galette, 1886

Oil on canvas · 15 × 18⅜″ · Berlin, Nationalgalerie

AFTER YEARS OF MATURATION AND DISILLUSION, including two stays in Paris as an apprentice art dealer, an abortive attempt to become a clergyman, and a desperate search for a place that would grant him the human environment and visual stimuli his work needed in order to develop, van Gogh settled in Paris in 1886. He met his brother, Théo, established there as an art dealer, in the Salon Carré of the Louvre. The two men began a common life in which difficult times, tensions, poverty, and Vincent's bouts of insanity were only offset by Théo's unlimited generosity and understanding of his brother's genius.

The van Goghs lived on the rue Lepic, a steep street leading up to Montmartre, then a picturesque village that attracted many young artists. Van Gogh arrived in Paris having created a significant, if awkward and sometimes eccentric, body of work of which only his brother and a few friends were aware. Vincent himself was conscious of his limitations and yearned to mature on Parisian soil. He wanted to learn both from academic sources and from the example of the avant-garde painters. He entered the studio of Cormon at the Ecole des Beaux-Arts, and his brother introduced him to the work of the impressionists, which Théo handled on a modest scale.

Van Gogh reacted to impressionism in a most particular way. Responsive to personal affinities rather than to general trends, he was more attracted to minor impressionist painters such as Guillaumin, whom he knew, or Raffaëlli than to Monet or Renoir. During his Parisian years, his paintings became generally lighter and more refined, his use of drawing more economical and expressive. This painting is an early work of his Parisian period and has all the qualities of an unpretentious oil study. The composition is still centered, the impasto heavy, and the black areas are still used as structure and accent, but its airiness and swiftness of execution prefigure the painter's later achievements.

The Asnières Bridges, 1887

Oil on canvas · 20½ × 25½″ · Zürich, E.G. Bührle Collection

Unfortunately, van Gogh's most formative years, his Parisian period, are poorly documented. Living with his brother, he hardly communicated with other members of his family or the few friends he had in Belgium and Holland. The intricate net of relationships with other artists, the nature of these friendships, their intensity, the exchange of ideas, and what van Gogh actually responded to can only be guessed or gathered through the writings of some other artists. His work of the time bears many influences: the discovery of impressionism—less the work of the first generation than the paintings of perhaps slightly minor but conscientious artists—and the revelation of pointillism, which van Gogh adopted for a short time and from which he drew important lessons but could not understand as a universal dogma. It is more likely that the most fruitful exchanges between van Gogh and other artists took place during "painting parties" along the rivers, or in suburban Paris.

Like many other painters, for a while he adopted the city as a subject matter. He responded particularly to Seurat's renditions of sunny afternoons in public places, a river bank, or an island, and some of his paintings of that period share this kind of subject. Views of bridges over the Seine were particularly favored by van Gogh. Psychological explanations have been given for this choice, but the aesthetic formulation of the theme seems more important. In this picture, the most fully achieved of the group, van Gogh successfully explores an intricate spatial relationship: The picture does not have a focal point. It is balanced instead between a vertical construction—from the rowboats on the river to the train on the bridge—and a receding one, which pulls the attention past the bridges toward the faint line of the factories in the background. This complex composition is reinforced by a finely defined use of colors, all bathed in a golden light and equally applied. The red figure of the woman seen from behind is not only a delightful impressionist touch, but in the absence of a focal point, it also serves infallibly to attract our eye.

Still Life of Shoes, 1886–1887

Oil on canvas · 19¼ × 28¼″ · Cambridge, Massachusetts, Fogg Art Museum
Bequest of Maurice Wertheim

EAGER TO LEARN AND TO IMPROVE HIS STYLE, van Gogh arrived in Paris to become a modern painter. For him more than for any other artist, modernism was a wide road paved with the examples of figures of the recent past—Corot, Daubigny, and Millet—and of the present. Among his contemporaries, van Gogh not only appreciated the work of the impressionists, he also admired the dark and sparkling still lifes of Monticelli, the peasant paintings of Jules Breton, and the works of the young painters who departed from strict impressionism. The production of his Parisian years reflects these multiple influences. It also occasionally reveals his struggle to adopt a modern idiom while maintaining his strict code of ethics, his "honesty" and the aesthetic creed of the Nuenen period.

Paradoxically, his subject matter became more conventional and increasingly limited to the disengaged topics of the impressionists: portraits, landscapes, still lifes. Yet within these limits, van Gogh introduced amazing innovations. His series of still lifes of shoes, for instance, is unprecedented in the history of painting. Inelegant and worn, they lack symbolic or decorative connotations. Yet they are painted with the same humanistic passion as the faces or hands of the Nuenen peasants. Nothing interferes with the brutal presentation of the subject. The earthy tones of the Nuenen period reappear here, and like the figures in *The Potato Eaters*, these humble objects are passive witnesses, not heroes, of the human condition.

Factories at Clichy, 1887

Oil on canvas · 27¼ × 28¾" · St. Louis Art Museum

VAN GOGH ONCE WROTE THAT HE ADMIRED Millet's peasants because they seemed to be painted with the very soil they ploughed. Texture and colors often had for him a symbolic meaning, and he eventually associated colors with the expression of specific emotions.

In Paris, however, van Gogh painted differently. His views of the city, streets, restaurants, and factories never comment on social situations. Their realism functions exclusively as the expression of an atmosphere. Van Gogh learned from the impressionists to dissociate himself from his subject matter, and *Factories at Clichy*, for instance, is astonishing in the complete detachment with which the scene is represented. Van Gogh's friend, the painter Emile Bernard, nevertheless thought that this painting "smelled of coal and gas."

The painting is considerably different from pure impressionist landscapes. The composition in three tiers—fields, factories, and sky—has an almost geometrical precision foreign to the improvised aspect of impressionist canvases. The straightforward view is typical of van Gogh, and it finds no equivalent among the impressionists. Finally, the colors do not achieve an all-over pattern but remain confined to the different areas they fill. This allows van Gogh to create an almost abstract image in which the heavy greenish sky, painted in broad strokes, is opposed to the energetic movement of the yellow field. Only the red roofs of the factories bring a joyful and permanent note.

Still Life with Books and Plaster Cast, 1887

Oil on canvas · 21½ × 18¼″ · Otterlo, Rijksmuseum Kröller-Müller

DISAPPOINTED BY THE ACADEMIC TEACHING OF HIS PROFESSOR, Fernand Cormon, van Gogh never returned to his studio after its reopening in 1887. In a letter to Emile Bernard, he said that "in the studios one not only does not learn much about painting, but not even much good about the art of living." In this still life, executed after he had left the studio, the juxtaposition of the objects seems to indicate the direction in which he intended to conduct his life. The sculpture—an academic plaster cast Cormon's students were asked to draw from (many paintings by van Gogh of the same sculpture still survive)—represents the classical tradition. It is eloquently juxtaposed with the realist tradition—symbolized by the novels of Guy de Maupassant and the Goncourt brothers—and the flowers, which stand for nature, ultimately van Gogh's only model.

More advanced than any academic model he could have followed, the still life also marks a breakthrough in van Gogh's own development. Since his first days in Paris and under the influence of the impressionists and the pointillists, he had adopted a fragmented brushstroke, but he suddenly turns to more solid shapes and a more directly expressive manner. The canvas is not treated any longer like a reflecting surface for optical plays; instead, van Gogh stresses its structure by a superimposition of solid shapes: All objects are placed on a background of off-white and yellow colors, which cannot be identified as objects but relate to the components of the still life, both in texture and color. The cast is of the same color as the layer under the books; the ocher book intensifies the straw-colored background, while the blue book plays the same role in the upper right corner. Even the harmonies of the rose branch, pink and green, are repeated in the strangely decorative fringes placed next to it, and to a lesser extent in the shadow of the books.

Portrait of Père Tanguy, 1887

Oil on canvas · 18½ × 15⅛″ · Athens, Stavros Niarchos Collection

THE ADMIRATION FOR JAPANESE PRINTS WAS CONSIDERABLE among artists of the late nineteenth century, and van Gogh was not the first painter to include them in the backgrounds of his portraits. They appear in paintings by Manet, Degas, and even Alfred Stevens, as commentaries upon the refined taste of their sitters (among them Zola and Tissot). Van Gogh uses them decoratively behind the figure of a man whose appearance and lifestyle were not much different from the peasants of Nuenen.

Père Tanguy, a sympathetic figure of the Parisian art world, sold canvases and colors in a little shop on the rue Clauzel, near Place Pigalle. Pissarro, Cézanne, Gauguin, and van Gogh were among his customers. A man of radical convictions (he had taken part in the Commune of 1870), he must have sensed intuitively that these young artists, rejected by the establishment, were close to him and that the political fight he had participated in was not entirely different from their own struggle to achieve recognition. He personally had little feeling for art, but because these artists exhibited in his shop and gave him canvases, or sold them cheaply to him, he became, by today's standards, one of the most important collectors of the avant-garde art of his time.

As in a self-portrait done in 1887 (now in the Rijksmuseum, Amsterdam), van Gogh contours the figure of the sitter with a red line, which isolates him both physically and psychologically from his background. This curious collagelike technique is also effective in that it allows van Gogh to treat the figure of Père Tanguy in an altogether different manner and spirit, without having to make subtle transitions.

Like the figure of a medieval saint, the sturdy figure of Père Tanguy sits surrounded by his attributes—here, paintings and prints. An eloquent contrast is made between his rugged face—with its intense eyes set far apart and its wide mouth—and the made-up faces of the Japanese actors in the prints by Hiroshige and Hokusai. This juxtaposition reflects van Gogh's double attachment to elevated forms of art and to the human soundness found in someone like Père Tanguy. His belief in an aesthetic that would convey deep ethical feelings was profound and is expressed here with absolute frankness.

Drawbridge near Arles (Pont de Langlois), 1888

Oil on canvas · 21¼ × 25⅝″ · Otterlo, Rijksmuseum Kröller-Müller

PARADOXICALLY, ONE OF THE SITES VAN GOGH WAS MOST FOND OF around Arles had a direct relationship to his native Holland. This drawbridge, and ten others, had been recently built over a small canal by a Dutch engineer. Its construction was similar to those of many bridges in the Dutch countryside. For van Gogh, however, it did not have a nostalgic character. The shape of the bridge happened to fit his search for a weightless world, a world of pure sensations and colors that he associated with Japan.

The composition of the picture still owes much to van Gogh's idea of Japonism: the bridge itself has the light and fragile quality of the wooden constructions one sees in Japanese prints. The contempt for traditional perspective increases the oriental feeling of the picture: The carriage and horse, for instance, are dwarfed but are important to the whole balance of the composition.

Above all, van Gogh executed this picture with complete sureness of hand and precision of vision. Blues dominate the picture, from the plain, screenlike sky to the fragmented rendition of the water; they also appear strangely reflected on the inner wall of the bridge and in the imbricated mosaic of colors that constitute the texture of the bridge itself.

Poetic and serene, this simple image of peacefulness appealed to van Gogh. He repeated it several times—not to study, like Monet, the variations of the light at different times, but to apprehend its permanent and "real character."

Portrait of a Zouave Bugler, 1888

Oil on canvas · 25⁹/₁₆ × 21¼″ · Amsterdam, Rijksmuseum Vincent van Gogh

IN VAN GOGH'S PORTRAITS, notably in those of his Arles period, force and expressiveness replace the qualities usually linked with this genre: exact likeness and understanding of the model's psychology. Searching for permanence in human types, he sought "simple" sitters—soldiers, a postman, working-class women.

In the portrait of this zouave (an Algerian infantryman in the old French army) to whom he had probably been introduced by his friend Milliet, himself a zouave lieutenant, an absence of personal expression contrasts with a deliberately exuberant play of colors, as if all the individuality of the model could be found in his uniform.

Van Gogh was delighted to find this model: "I have a model at last . . . a lad with a small face, with the neck of a bull, and the eye of a tiger." Impressed by his physical presence, he translated it in a "savage combination of incongruous tones." The heavy, squarish head is repeated in the square pattern of the door and bricks behind him. This remarkably abstract and rigorous background forms an appropriate setting for the convoluted play of the embroidered spirals on the zouave's jacket. These volutes introduce the only vertical and decorative elements in an otherwise sternly parallel division of the canvas.

The simplification of the colors make this picture—and the other versions van Gogh did of it—a "loud" portrait. Conscious of the exaggerations and deformations in these portraits, he also called them "ugly," but he added that he "should like to be always working in common . . . portraits, like this."

Fishing Boats on the Beach, 1888

Oil on canvas · 25⅜ × 31⅞″ · Amsterdam, Rijksmuseum Vincent van Gogh

VAN GOGH'S EXOTIC VISION OF THE SOUTH was not disappointed by his first encounter with the Mediterranean, which, in his words, had "the colors of mackerel, changeable." And he added, "You don't always know if it is green or violet, you can't even say it's blue, because the next moment, the changing light has taken on a tinge of rose or gray." From Arles, van Gogh had gone to Saintes-Maries where he painted several studies of boats on the beach. The graceful lines of these sailboats with their thin, colored masts give the composition an elegant airiness, which, surprisingly, is not evident in the rendition of the immaterial elements, such as the sky or the sea. These are painted with a delicacy that does not exclude strength. The changing nature of the water, especially as strikes the shore, is translated in opalescent pinks and light greens. The sky itself is a vibrating texture of closely juxtaposed blues and silvery grays.

From Saintes-Maries, van Gogh wrote to his brother that he was "convinced of the importance . . . of absolutely piling on or exaggerating the colors." This he does particularly in the flat, colorful surfaces of the boats, so texturally different from the sand, water, and sky. *Amitié*, friendship, the name of one of the boats, stands out prominently in the center of the picture. This genuinely personal touch—perhaps a sign of van Gogh's need for companionship—is echoed by the signature, "Vincent," on the diaphanous stele, like the few words of a Japanese haiku.

View of Saintes-Maries, 1888

Oil on canvas · 25⅛ × 20⅞″ · Otterlo, Rijksmuseum Kröller-Müller

SAINTES-MARIES-DE-LA-MER, A SMALL TOWN in the Camargue where van Gogh went to see the effect of the blue sky on the Mediterranean, reminded him oddly of Holland. To Théo he wrote: ''The chief building after the old church and an ancient fortress, is the barracks. And the houses—like the ones on our heaths and peat bogs in Drenthe.'' The revealing light of the South reminded him, too, of the icy luminosity seen both in the Dutch countryside and the landscapes of Dutch seventeenth-century artists. Van Gogh does not follow the example of Philips Koninck in this view of the town, as he does in his landscape of the Crau (see *Plaine de la Crau*), but he details the city, silhouetted against the sky, with a precision similar to Vermeer's in his *View of Delft*.

More topographic than most of his landscapes, this view avoids banality thanks to van Gogh's almost obsessive need to paint, above all, the light. The plain and solid sky is painted with enough white in it to suggest the power of the sun and its blinding effect, and the field is a rich and luscious combination of greens and lavenders. Both the field, with its color streaks, and the plain sky enhance the imbrication of closely related hues, which form the geometric structure of the town punctuated in the foreground by the darker lines of the cowherds' cottages.

Wheatfield with Sower, 1888

Oil on canvas · 25¼ × 31¹¹/₁₆″ · Otterlo, Rijksmuseum Kröller-Müller

MILLET'S *SOWER* HAD OBSESSED VAN GOGH'S IMAGINATION since he had copied it while in the Borinage in 1880. The heroic figure of the lonesome peasant at work in his field embodied qualities van Gogh was seeking to achieve in his own paintings: dedication, perserverance, arduous labor.

Inhibited by the power of Millet's image, van Gogh borrowed it without changes in several drawings and oil studies. Yet he felt that he could somehow improve on it: "I have been longing to do a sower for such a long time, but the things I've wanted for a long time never come off. And so I am almost afraid of it. And yet, after Millet and Lhermitte, what still remains to be done is—a sower, in color and large sizes."

This *Wheatfield with Sower* is the first work in a series of compositions that present this peasant not as an isolated figure, following Millet's example, but as a man taking part in the cycle of life. This is achieved through a visionary conception of landscape in which the wide field, the setting sun, and the path leading toward it have a mysterious, cosmic, and almost ritualistic significance.

In many ways, this painting differs from the exuberant ones at Arles. Its seriousness and philosophical implications prefigure the artist's later works.

Haystacks in Provence, 1888

Oil on canvas · 28¾ × 36⅜″ · Otterlo, Rijksmuseum Kröller-Müller

As SEASONS WENT BY, VAN GOGH NEVER CEASED to be amazed by the changing of colors in Provence: "It has become very different from what it was in Spring," he wrote at the time he was working on this picture, "and yet I have certainly no less love for this countryside, burnt up as it begins to be from now on. Everywhere now there is gold, bronze, copper, one might say, and this with the green azure of the sky blanched with heat: a delicious color, extraordinarily harmonious, with the blended tones of Delacroix."

The massive haystacks, like mountains of gold, communicate their radiance to the entire picture. A glowing light, coming from the left, illuminates every part of it; it details the texture of the ricks, casting on the right one a soft shadow that complements the bright gold of the larger one. On closer examination, the painting reveals a multiplicty of colors, distributed in an almost pointillist technique, especially in the darker areas, so finely nuanced. With great mastery, van Gogh balances the colors; the green of the lower corner is, for instance, repeated in the wonderful green shutters of the house in the upper left corner. Blues are not limited to the thickly painted sky but appear, also, in the house between the two haystacks, and, in lighter touches, on the rocks in the bottom left of the canvas. This sureness of rapport between colors does not betray painstaking planning but, on the contrary, a great enthusiasm for the subject and a rapid, sensitive execution in which improvisation and immediate response to shapes and colors are the best means of expression.

Sunflowers, 1888

Oil on canvas · 37⅜ × 28¾" · London, The National Gallery

THE PAINTINGS OF SUNFLOWERS WERE PART of the decorative scheme van Gogh had devised for his house in Arles. He wanted them to stand "like candelabras" around the *Portrait of Madame Roulin*. Flowers were scarce in Provence, but van Gogh was extremely fond of these sunflowers, which he had to get up early in order to see in full bloom. Because of this, he felt they participated in a natural, or cosmic, cycle and celebrated the sun and life. Their bright color was particularly appealing to van Gogh, who had discovered the power of gold and yellow in the South: "Now we're having a gloriously strong windless heat here, which suits me well. A sun, a light that for want of a better word I can only call yellow, pale sulphur yellow, pale gold lemon. How beautiful yellow is!"

This bouquet of sunflowers does not have the prettiness of a composed impressionist bouquet. Instead, it is an almost barbaric celebration of life, a pagan worship of the sun. The presentation is direct, and does not research any effect beyond the blunt expression of basic joy. The quasi monochrome of the picture is extraordinary: From pale lemon to deep orange, all tones of yellow are represented on each individual flower, on the vase, and on the simple background, itself affected by this colorful exuberance. A fine blue line, complementary to the yellow, is delicately drawn and reappears in the signature. Green, the combination of both colors, adds another high-keyed note to the picture. A touch of white on the vase is an elegant detail, which makes the whole canvas glow.

The Postman Roulin, 1888

Oil on canvas · 31⅞ × 25⅝″ · Boston, The Museum of Fine Arts

PORTRAITURE WAS A CONSIDERABLE CHALLENGE for avant-garde artists of the late nineteenth century. More criticized than any other genre, it incurred the risk of displeasing sitters and public alike. Portraits commissioned from artists like Degas, for instance, were usually rejected or else received with cold indifference. As a result, these artists preferred painting each other or a carefully selected group of friends and supporters.

Van Gogh "felt confident when . . . doing portraits, knowing that that work has much more depth." One of the tragedies of his life was his lack of suitable models. In Arles, having severed himself from the Parisian art community, he again took popular types for models. Among those, the Roulin family became close friends and privileged sitters. The head of the family was a postman, "a Republican like Tanguy" with "a head like Socrates." Van Gogh did several portraits of him, always wearing, like the zouave bugler, his bright uniform.

The simplicity of the picture is made effective by a rigorous, almost geometrical construction. A series of strong triangles establish its armature: the points of the beard, the lapels, the white shirt, the position of the legs. This play of triangular shapes, however, does not hide the physical presence of the body—strong and lively—underscored by the black lines, which create natural rhythmic accents on the otherwise plain blue surface.

Still Life with Books and Oleanders, 1888

Oil on canvas · 23⅝ × 28¾″ · New York City, The Metropolitan Museum of Art

THE NOVELIST AND ESSAYIST EMILE ZOLA was among van Gogh's favorite writers. Unlike most avant-garde artists, van Gogh was less taken by Zola's astute criticism than by his naturalist novels from which he often quoted relevant parts in his letters to his brother Théo.

In this still life, van Gogh pairs judiciously a novel by Zola with a sumptuous bouquet. These exuberant flowers provide a natural counterpart to the title of the novel, *La Joie de Vivre* (Joy of Living). "Friendship" and "joy of living" are words that appear around this time in van Gogh's paintings and reveal his hopes for his new life at Arles.

Even without the help of the painted words, this still life breathes a strong and confident spirit. The brushwork is firm and decisive, the colors enticing. The same energy and vitality displayed in his contemporary portraits and landscapes can be perceived here. Above all, van Gogh revels in distributing colors with absolute brio. His mastery of details, such as the red edge of the table, or its animated surface of pink, mauve, and light green dashes, does not amount to a gratuitous approach to painting but displays, on the contrary, his refined sense for a calculated and sensitive balance of components.

Compared to the energetic surface of the table and the odd perspective of the books, the bouquet of oleanders appears remarkably calm and radiant. The interwoven pattern of the leaves, with its superimposition of light and dark greens, fulfills the same function as the masts of the sailboats in his picture of *Fishing Boats on the Beach*: It creates an armature around which the space of the painting becomes a luminous and tangible surface.

Portrait of Patience Escalier, 1888

Oil on canvas · 27¾ × 22¾″ · London, Chester Beatty Collection

"WHAT A MISTAKE PARISIANS MAKE IN NOT HAVING A PALATE for crude things," wrote van Gogh to his brother. In the letter, he told him that he should expect to receive this portrait of a peasant from Provence. "You are shortly to make the acquaintance of Master Patience Escalier, a sort of 'man with a hoe,' formerly cowherd of the Camargue, now gardener at a house in the Crau. The coloring of this peasant portrait is not so black as in the 'Potato Eaters.'" Van Gogh's Nuenen peasants were made of the dark earth and gray sky of the North. Patience Escalier reflects the colors of the South. The blue of the sky, the bright oranges and yellows of the sun-drenched fields, and the pale soil of the South are literally translated in this figure. Sturdy qualities, associated with the peasant's rugged life, his honesty, and his directness, do not preclude an insistence upon particular features, such as the haunting inquisitiveness of the expression and the astounding liveliness of the hands.

More than in any other portrait, van Gogh maintains here a balance between general and particular, simplicity and complexity, drawing and color. Upon examination, the "simplicity" of the image disappears to make way for a complex net of formal relationships that constitutes the armature of the picture. The composition is made effective by its play of triangles—the most obvious of all being the face, whose shape is reversed in that of the hat. It is also evident in the movement of the shoulders: the position of the hands forms arrows pointing toward the peasant's eyes—the focal point of the portrait. The seemingly limited palette is equally effective. Blue and orange are not only the dominant and complementary colors; largely distributed over the background and the blouse, they reappear in tighter streaks in the face. The arbitrary use of red lines around the hat, the ears, and the eyes not only gives the face its vitality, it also links it to the red scarf and sleeves. Rarely has any artist succeeded so well in relating every part of a picture in order to stress its expressive quality.

Van Gogh often wondered how his impressionist friends would respond to the wild works he was doing in Provence. He wished, in fact, to show this portrait next to one by Toulouse-Lautrec. He thought that his picture "would gain by the odd juxtaposition"— placing it, that is, next to Lautrec's "powder and elegance."

The Artist's House at Arles, 1888

Oil on canvas · 30 × 37″ · Amsterdam, Rijksmuseum Vincent van Gogh

ALTHOUGH VAN GOGH'S REASONS FOR SETTLING at Arles rather than in another Southern city remain unknown, his hope for a place where he could create far from the dull light of the North and the competitive Parisian milieu are indicated in many letters. Aware of the isolation he endured in Nuenen, he was eager to set up a colony of artists: "Here there will always be artists coming and going, anxious to escape from the severity of the North. And I think myself that I shall always be one of them." He first met artists who, like him, were foreigners—English, Danish, and American—but he immediately sought to invite Gauguin, who was then at Pont-Aven.

In anticipation of the establishment of this colony, and above all of the arrival of Gauguin and of his own brother, Théo, he rented a small house that he intended to become a center for the new group of painters. To make its interior of white-washed walls and red-tiled floors more enticing—it reminded him of a painting by the Dutch seventeenth-century artist Boosbom—he began an extensive decoration program. He wanted the house to look like "an artist's house—not precious, on the contrary, nothing precious, but everything from the chairs to the pictures having character." In contrast to the stillness of the interior, the exterior reminded him of Daumier or of descriptions of places in the novels of Emile Zola: loud and colorful. Although he found his task "frightfully difficult," he was eager to show his brother an accurate view of the house, hoping that it would encourage Théo to move in with him. This cityscape is, in fact, as precise in its conception as the views done by the Dutch seventeenth-century painters. Details such as the railroad bridge contribute to the reality of the situation. But van Gogh emphasizes the sharp contrast of colors and, believing in their magic power, expands the yellows—the color of friendship—to the surroundings of the house, under a sky of pure cobalt.

The Night Cafe, 1888

Oil on canvas · 37½ × 35″ · New Haven, Connecticut, Yale University Art Gallery, Gift of Stephen C. Clark

"The cafe is a place where one can ruin oneself, go mad or commit a crime." In writing this sentence—as in executing this picture—van Gogh seemed to conjure the evil spirits that might have attracted him to this place, a night establishment close to his house on Place Lamartine in Arles. In van Gogh's mind the intent of the picture was moralizing, and he wrote extensively about its significance. He found it "ugly"—perhaps more intellectually than esthetically—and gave it to his landlord in lieu of rent. The cafe was a low-class establishment, similar to those frequented in Paris by Toulouse-Lautrec or the young Picasso. Prostitutes and drunks were its main customers, yet van Gogh's description of the place is not explicit. In that respect, and because of its symbolic overtones, it differs readily from the work of these other painters. Eloquently, the painting centers not around a main figure but focuses instead on a general atmosphere made tangible by a scattering of objects bathed in a light similar to the "pale sulphur" of "a devil's furnace." The lack of center in the picture corresponds metaphorically to the dissolute life of the customers, sunk in loneliness and related only to a world of objects. The empty chairs, tables with leftover bottles and glasses, the mirror, and the clock all express the desolation of the place. Most of these objects—mirror, clock, game—are traditionally associated with *vanitas* pictures and are symbols of passing pleasures leading toward inevitable decay. The homely figure of the landlord in white stands like the leader of some medieval death dance upon whom the exaggerated perspective of the floor and the halos around the lamps create a diabolic movement.

Portrait of the Second Lieutenant Milliet, 1888

Oil on canvas · 23½ × 19¼″ · Otterlo, Rijksmuseum Kröller-Müller

In Arles van Gogh had become friendly with an officer of the zouave regiment, Second Lieutenant Milliet, to whom he gave drawing lessons. Fascinated by his personality and intrigued by his considerable successes with women, van Gogh rapidly decided to execute his portrait. Milliet was a poor model, but the artist wrote: ''. . . he is a good-looking boy, very unconcerned and easy-going in his behavior, and he would suit me damned well for the picture of a lover.'' It is indeed the alert bon vivant rather than the hero who had won his medals in Tonkin whom van Gogh chose to represent. The portrait is full of sympathy and humor. It strikes a different note from other contemporary portraits in that the background is a richly animated surface, suitable for the portrait of a man full of vitality. The vibrant pattern of this background also restates the decorative embroideries on the uniform's jacket and befits the lively undulation of the outline of the face as well as the amusing tilt of the kepi. The painterliness of the background might also be a witty comment upon Milliet's opinion of van Gogh's painting: although he took drawing lessons from him and admired his ability as a draughtsman, he thought poorly of him as a painter and would occasionally argue with him about his wild use of colors.

Another delightful detail in the picture is the emblem of the French troops in Africa, the star and quarter moon in the upper right corner; it recalls the crests of the noble sitters in formal portraits of the seventeenth century and, at the same time, comments humorously upon van Gogh's fascination with stars and celestial bodies, both of which appear at this time in his work.

Portrait of the Artist's Mother, 1888

Oil on canvas · 16 × 12¾" · Pasadena, California, Norton Simon Museum

VINCENT VAN GOGH'S MOTHER, Anna-Cordelia Carbentus, was a remarkable woman; she was a fluent letter-writer as well as an amateur watercolorist. Born in 1819, she died in 1907, after having survived her three sons and her husband, whom she often helped in his duties as pastor of their community.

This portrait was painted at Arles after a black-and-white photograph van Gogh could not suffer because of its lack of color. It is the only portrait of a relative van Gogh ever painted. The artist enjoyed the idea of working from a photograph: "Ah, what portraits could be made from nature with photography and painting! I always hope that we are still to have a great revolution in portraiture." Although van Gogh abandoned his original idea to paint his mother's dress carmine, he limited his coloring to a strong contrast of simple light and dark colors—the most stunning of which is the plain green background—which enhances the radiance of her expression. Perhaps because of its relationship to the original photograph, the portrait is one of the most naturalistic in van Gogh's oeuvre. He does not seek any effect but paints a familiar face, which is, above all, a generous smile and a haunting glance.

Van Gogh still attempts to express in his portraits the essential qualities of his models. The subtle balance of intimacy and filial complicity is offset by the lyricism of the colors and the boldness of the brushwork. These transform the particular features of his mother into an archetypal image.

The Sower, 1888

Oil on canvas · 12¾ × 15¾″ · Amsterdam, Rijksmuseum Vincent van Gogh

WHETHER IN PARIS OR IN THE SOUTH, van Gogh usually chose his subjects from among his immediate surroundings. So eager was he to discover new stimuli—a new light and new colors—that he left Paris for the South. A picture like *The Sower* is disconcerting only if placed in the context of his contemporary production: painted at Arles, it does not reflect in any way his astonishment at the colors of the South. In fact, in painting it van Gogh was reaching the culmination of a theme that had preoccupied him since he had encountered the subject in the work of J. F. Millet. The image of the peasant laboring in his field was particularly appealing to van Gogh, for it represented his ideal of human participation in the cosmic cycle of life. His fascination with the subject is first apparent in numerous literal copies after Millet's sower. Particularly when he was in the South, he rapidly broadened the theme by including the figure in a symbolically evocative landscape and by relinquishing Millet's muddy palette in favor of a brilliant, if unorthodox one.

The painting was, according to van Gogh himself, his first serious effort to use color as a "very prominent part." Although the colors are limited, they are extraordinarily effective, and their arbitrariness is skillfully related to the expressive character of the picture.

Van Gogh achieves here a horizontal composition in two equal parts. The attention devoted to the upper part, the sky, recalls northern, and particularly German, painters who, from Altdorfer to Caspar-David Friedrich, used this device to express a sense of awe before the infinite. The most spectacular element in the sky—beside its own color, which is as wild as those van Gogh puts behind his portraits—is the enormous sun, heavily painted and whose texture seems to indicate a swirling movement. The sun, acting almost as a halo above the head of the peasant, is the key to the picture in which it presides like the figure of a god over an altar. The accentuated perspective, leading to a point slightly off the left center of the picture, as well as the rendition of the soil in rapid, small dabs, suggests an acceleration of the very movement of the earth. Painted in close hues, the solid and dark shapes of the peasant and of the tree seem to fight helplessly against the menacing motion of these cosmic forces.

Portrait of Madame Ginoux (L'Arlésienne), 1888

Oil on canvas · 35⅜ × 28⅜" · New York City, The Metropolitan Museum of Art
Samuel A. Lewisohn Bequest

AFTER SEVERAL MONTHS OF REPEATED EFFORTS, van Gogh finally succeeded in convincing Gauguin to leave Pont-Aven and to move in with him in Arles. At first their companionship could not have been more successful: the two painters delighted in the same subjects, painted together, and enjoyed each other's company. Van Gogh's dream of setting up an art community seemed happily to be coming true.

Among the models the two artists shared was Madame Ginoux, a typical Arlésienne who with her husband ran the Café de la Gare, not far from van Gogh's "yellow house." Van Gogh "slashed out (the portrait) in an hour." Gauguin's influence can be detected in the flat rendition of shapes—for instance, in the optical play that delineates the space around the right arm of the sitter. Also unusual for van Gogh is the attitude of the model; she is caught in a pensive mood, in the midst of her reading. This spontaneous and dreamy image contrasts with the rigid and posed fixity of his other portraits of the period. But typical of him is the expression of a mood through a combination of colors, which is not only arbitrary, but contrary to one's expectations. Here, the yellow background, unexpected in an evocation of revery, has a luminous intensity, which is that of the South—and therefore reflects an otherwise immaterial exterior world—and which, with more subtlety and by contrast with the black dress and hair, expresses the spiritual life of Madame Ginoux.

Evocative, too, of medieval gold-ground pictures, the portrait has a refined and aristocratic beauty, an elegance noticeable in the fine features of the model: the sharp nose, thin mouth, and delicately drawn eyebrows, repeated in the peaks of the dress and shawl. The still life of books, with its unusual colors, relates to the fine touches of pale green, pink and reds in the scarf and face. Unlike other books in different works by van Gogh, they do not explicitly comment upon the mood of the painting but are objects of meditation, like modern books of hours.

Portrait of Armand Roulin, 1888

Oil on canvas · 25⅝ × 21¼″ · Essen, Folkwang Museum

IN ORDER TO RENDER THE SOFT AND IMPRECISE FEATURES of this adolescent boy—Armand Roulin, the postman's son, was only seventeen at the time—van Gogh adopted a fluid, almost languid, style. The portrait has an informal presence, conveyed by the most minute details: the slight slant of the sitter's position, his evasive glance, the sensuous movement of the lips, even the tilted hat. These details, the swift drawing and almost watercolorlike technique concur to create an image that is not based on sound geometry but on a juxtaposition of individual characteristics. Nevertheless the portrait owes its coherence to a subtle use of colors. The hazy tones—from the pale lemon coat to the bluish background—share a common softness and low-keyed atmosphere. Van Gogh's carefully constricted palette, with its elegant balance of grayish blues and lighter hues, enhances the face, equally delicate, which is highlighted by two small touches of paint in the eyes.

Van Gogh's amazing ability to communicate a richness of situation through a simple portrait is best exemplified here. On close examination, the portrait reveals a sunny airiness and an atmospheric transparence that are usually conveyed only in landscapes. Paradoxically, van Gogh seems to dominate his "loud" portraits. Facing youth and humble grace, he responds to it with exquisite sensibility and delicacy of approach.

Van Gogh's Chair and Pipe, 1888–89

Oil on canvas · 35½ × 28″ · London, The Trustees of the Tate Gallery

VAN GOGH'S PREDILECTION FOR UNUSUAL STILL-LIFE MATTER is evident once again in this surprising image of his own chair. The painting, one of a pair (see *Gauguin's Armchair*), was executed the day before his quarrel with Gauguin.

The sturdiness of the image, the tangible materiality of the chair, make the moral emptiness of the composition even more poignant. The homely still life of ghostly pipe and white tobacco pouch within the larger still life of the chair stresses the desolate spirit of the picture. Once previously van Gogh had associated these objects with remembrance of the dead. Shortly after his father had died, in 1885, he had represented his father's pipe and pouch—his constant companions—along with flowers.

Although it may have been prompted by his disenchantment with Gauguin's presence in Arles, the picture does not speak in anecdotal terms. The collapse of van Gogh's dreams is nothing compared to what is expressed here: an anguishing mystery, a metaphysical void rather than merely human absence.

The composition ignores traditional perspective. The floating of the chair against a background of solid elements—tiles, door, or wall—gives it its individuality. Its neatly outlined design relates only in a dizzying way to the pattern of the tiles and the geometry of the door with its painted line. Alive in the midst of the rigorous design of the room, it may signify indirectly an expression of personal freedom among rivalries and hostile surroundings. Massive and obtrusive, too, it stands in the picture as incongruously as does the work itself among the happy products of van Gogh's Arles period, a menacing prelude to self-destruction, insanity, and suicide.

Gauguin's Armchair, 1888

Oil on canvas · 35¾ × 28¾″ · Amsterdam, Rijksmuseum Vincent van Gogh

SHORTLY BEFORE THE STORMY NIGHT THAT PROMPTED his departure from Arles, Gauguin had written to Theo van Gogh that he and Vincent "simply couldn't live together in peace because of incompatibility of temper." Although van Gogh himself was less aware of this incompatibility, he could not ignore their divergences of opinion. Their characters were opposite: They liked different artists — van Gogh was still under the spell of the Barbizon school, whereas Gauguin was more responsive to the flat and precise drawing of Ingres and Degas — and they were linked more by a similar dedication to their own work than by common views or profound bonds of friendship.

This picture, a "portrait" of a chair, was conceived of as one of a pair (see *Van Gogh's Chair*). In it van Gogh intuitively made explicit these antagonistic worlds. The picture of his own chair is solid and rustic, that of Gauguin's more refined, more "beautiful." The lack of human presence is not so painful here, for it is a "night effect" and the lights — on the chair and on the wall — bring a consoling, hopeful note. For the spatial ambiguity, the claustrophobic corner of his own room, van Gogh substitutes in Gauguin's chamber a simply defined space. A clear line separates the floor from the wall and opens up the composition laterally. The curvilinear armchair — somewhat evocative of Gauguin's decorative patterns — has a sprightly liveliness, as does the floor rendered in sparkling dashes.

Van Gogh never painted a straightforward portrait of Gauguin. Yet this oblique "portrait" reveals more than an ordinary likeness: the subject is transcended. In the very essence of things, shapes, and colors associated in van Gogh's mind with Gauguin, the artist tells us about his admiration, his hope, and perhaps his deceptiveness toward his friend.

Still Life, 1889

Oil on canvas · 19¾ × 25¼″ · Otterlo, Rijksmuseum Kröller-Müller

TRAGEDY BROKE AT ARLES ON DECEMBER 24, 1888, when van Gogh, in a bout of insanity and suffering a high fever, threatened Gauguin with a knife, then cut off part of his own ear. Rescued by the postman Roulin, he was treated at the city hospital. A few days later, still recovering from his wound, Vincent wrote Théo that he would soon start working again and that he would "begin by doing one or two still lifes so as to get back into the habit of painting."

Still lifes, self-portraits, reassuring images, such as sunflowers, constitute van Gogh's production during his recovery (January, 1889). This choice of close-to-home subjects stresses van Gogh's superhuman effort to recapture contact with reality. For a while his pictures became inquisitive reassessments of familiar objects. In this still life, in particular, van Gogh represented once again objects he had associated with himself and Gauguin while painting their respective chairs: the pouch, the pipe, the candle, a book — in this instance a medical treatise, which probably belonged to van Gogh's physician, Dr. Rey. The proliferation of things on the table, whether placed on the drawing board or on the red edge (such as the gigantic water pitcher) makes their individual presence less menacing. Juxtaposed and unrelated, they are like the letters of an alphabet van Gogh tries to recompose. The high-spirited colors and improvised composition give the picture an appealing casualness.

Van Gogh's only link with the outside world, a letter addressed to him — probably by his brother, who had come to Arles immediately after the tragedy but had had to return to Paris — is well displayed and wittily constitutes reversed signature in the lower right corner of the canvas.

Portrait of Madame Roulin (La Berceuse), 1889

Oil on canvas · 36⅝ × 28⅞″ · The Art Institute of Chicago,
Helen Birch Bartlett Collection

THE WIFE OF THE POSTMAN ROULIN was a maternal figure in van Gogh's life. After the crisis during which he cut off his ear, she and her husband took care of him. Van Gogh executed several portraits of this woman rocking the cradle. The concentration of her attitude and her dignified appearance recall those of a medieval saint. In fact, van Gogh wanted to create a popular image that would produce the same soothing effect as the chromolithographs uneducated people were fond of hanging on their walls.

Impressed by the recent reading of Pierre Loti's *Pêcheurs d'Islande*, he said that he had "the idea of executing a picture in which sailors, who are children and martyrs, seeing it in the cabin of their boat, should feel the old sense of cradling come over them and remember their old lullabies." Van Gogh envisioned this picture as the center part of a polyptich whose other wings—three or four on each side—would be his series of sunflowers. These, he thought, would form "torches or candelabras" around the central iconlike figure of Madame Roulin.

The portrait was begun while Gauguin was still in Arles, and it reflects his influence in the wide, flat areas of colors and in the decorative background, which replaced the sternly uniform ones against which van Gogh usually set his models. Van Gogh paid extreme attention to the execution of this portrait, and of its other versions. He said of them that he knew very well "that it is neither drawn or painted as correctly as a Bouguereau" and regretted it because he had "an earnest desire to be correct." Van Gogh perhaps never achieved the correct likeness he was striving for, yet his portrait radiates with actual presence, psychological insight, and moral truthfulness.

Starry Night, 1889

Oil on canvas · 28¾ × 36¼" · New York City, The Museum of Modern Art,
Lillie P. Bliss Bequest

DURING VAN GOGH'S COMMITMENT AT SAINT-REMY-DE-PROVENCE a new vision of nature took place in his work. Relinquishing both the intimate naturalism of the paintings done around Arles and their sharp juxtaposition of colors, he produced canvases animated by a rhythmic energy, based partly on the different type of landscape he had for a model and also on the logical development of his own style. The contempt van Gogh had shown previously for spatial conventions resulted in strongly coherent images, where, for instance, sky and earth, rooftops and fields seem to share a common texture. Concurrently, his palette darkened or reached a deeper intensity, which often accounts for the tragic mood of these paintings.

In *Starry Night*, van Gogh's tendency to animate his landscape reaches a paroxysm and turns into an immensely poetic and visionary evocation of the night. In a previous painting, van Gogh had successfully treated the same theme, but still with elegance and restraint. The subject has now become an hallucinatory vision that owes its power to the presence of cosmic forces, felt in the swirling movement of the sky, the halos around the stars, and the celestial body—it is both moon and sun—on the right. The same presence and movement animate the mountainous landscape, which is swept along in this whirling of elements. The eye is led from the left to the right edge of the canvas and back to the center, in the midst of the coiling nebula. Dwarfed below this unfurling of stars and clouds is the village, with its square houses and church tower, which itself repeats the shape of the cypress tree. The buildings appear defenseless, and yet they contribute to the animation of the whole.

Many explanations have been advanced for this painting: expression of sheer madness or, perhaps, an illustration of apocalyptic symbols. We know that it was executed after a spell of religious hallucinations van Gogh endured. A religious man without being affiliated with a church, van Gogh still suffered from the frustration he had experienced years ago when he had discovered his inability to follow his father into the ministry. Conscious of his importance as an artist, he often looked at his work with humility and found the paintings of other artists far superior to his own efforts. Inhibition and frustration were serious components of his split personality. In *Starry Night*, where sky and earth, nature and man-made objects participate in the same cosmic adventure, van Gogh seems to recover with vehemence, and a sense of tragedy, the coherence that was lacking in his own mind.

Self-Portrait, 1889

Oil on canvas · 22⅜ × 17⅛" · New York City, John Hay Whitney Collection

VAN GOGH'S MASTERY OF PORTRAITURE and his conveying of a mood or psychological insight are always functions of a highly disciplined use of color. Whether in his Arles portraits, where the brilliant, plain backgrounds create the atmosphere, or in this one, where the texture and color of his blouse are hardly different from the background, the dominating tone and the parsimonious use of complementaries are the key to the picture's meaning.

This portrait was executed at Saint-Rémy, for "want of a better model." Yet in its obsessive workmanship, the attention given to the concentrated expression, and the odd general harmony, one senses van Gogh's fascination with his own emaciated image. The inquisitiveness of the expression and the peering of the blue eyes are the psychological and harmonic clues to the portrait.

The various ways in which the paint is applied and the direction of the brushstrokes diffuse or center the energy of the whole canvas so that this seemingly "simple" image can eventually be read as a sum of multiple components. Attention is naturally concentrated on the head, around which solid brushstrokes form a halo that broadens until it becomes parallel to the edge of the canvas. The finely chiseled face, with its gold and greens and its tighter net of fine strokes, appears as a ghostly presence. The blouse, with its longer and wider streaks, has a life of its own, and its texture recalls that of some of van Gogh's still lifes. The palette, however, with the brushes sprouting from it, has a solid consistency that also extends to the artist's thumb. Because of this diversity of techniques, the portrait achieves a liveliness and a sense of self-comprehension even more poignant than in many other self-portraits.

Hospital Ward at Arles, 1889

Oil on canvas · 29⅛ × 36¼″ · Winterthur, Sammlung Oskar Reinhart "Am Römerholz"

DURING HIS INTERNMENT AT SAINT-RÉMY, van Gogh suffered greatly from the lack of varied subject matter. Although nature had always been for him a fruitful source of inspiration, he had often expressed his need for models. The permission he had obtained to paint outside the hospital, under the surveillance of a hospital warden, was welcome but did not replace the sitters he had found in Arles. Even self-portraits were not sufficiently rewarding for van Gogh, who sought to express a wide range of human types and conditions. To compensate for this lack of subject matter, van Gogh turned to painting images that had struck his memory; eventually he executed copies after paintings he admired.

Because this painting was executed from memory, it does not have the immediacy of his contemporary landscapes. A tightly controlled handling of the brush betrays van Gogh's careful application to the reconstruction of an image. Devices employed in other paintings reappear in this one: the configuration of the room with its slanted floor and exaggerated perspective duplicates the claustrophobic feeling expressed in the *Night Cafe*. A repertoire of objects and attitudes, the lamp, the chair—curiously reminiscent of Gauguin's armchair—the figures isolated around the stove, like the potato eaters around their table, reveals the artist's obsession with these themes. Yet they appear here without the liveliness they had in their original settings. Likewise, the colors are more realistic, and van Gogh's technique harks back to an almost impressionist manner, which had been foreign to his work since his departure from Paris.

The Ravine of Les Peyroulets, 1889

Oil on canvas · 28⅜ × 36¼″ · Otterlo, Rijksmuseum Kröller-Müller

"THERE ARE MOMENTS WHEN NATURE IS SUPERB, autumn effects glorious in color, green skies contrasting with foliage in yellows, oranges, greens . . . heat-withered grass among which, however, the rains have given a last energy to certain plants." This description of the countryside van Gogh discovered on the occasional walk he was allowed to take during his confinement at Saint-Rémy seems to apply particularly to the painting of this ravine. Different from the countryside around Arles, van Gogh's new domain with its narrow paths among trees, the subtle shading of overgrown vegetation, and the convulsive shapes of rocks and olive trees was a projection of his tormented mind.

In the paintings of this period van Gogh generally relinquished the flat, Japanese juxtaposition of intense colors and the glowing stillness of his Arles paintings. Movement, translated into curvilinear shapes and spatially unsettling patterns, dominates his compositions. The energy of the graphism is no longer restricted to decorative schemes but is the core itself of the paintings. In *Les Peyroulets*, for instance, strong black lines design the armature of the composition—two bisecting diagonals—and are immediately echoed, repeated, and contradicted in a proliferation of smaller, lighter ones, which provide the painting with its staggering dynamism.

As drawing takes over, colors become more subtle. Van Gogh compared the sky of Saint-Rémy to "our skies in the North." Grays, blacks, and silvery tones blur the primary colors, parsimoniously used. The cold range of white to green tones in *Les Peyroulets* is animated only by the sparkling red and ocher of the flowers and the women's dresses.

The Drinkers (after Daumier), 1890

Oil on canvas · 23^{11}/$_{16}$ × 28¾″ · The Art Institute of Chicago,
The Joseph Winterbotham Collection

TO EXECUTE PAINTINGS AFTER PRINTS, whether by Millet or by Daumier, was for van Gogh not just a question of coloring these images, but of trying either to recreate what these artists did not have time to do or of simply inventing a colorful correspondence to what they had chosen to represent in black and white.

During the last months he spent at the asylum of Saint-Rémy, these copies, which he found "difficult to do," gave him a pleasurable challenge. Into them he occasionally introduced particular elements that were pertinent to his life: some faces are modeled after people van Gogh knew, and background landscapes are often related to the countryside of Saint-Rémy, which so fascinated him.

The choice of subjects is also revealing. Besides Millet's peasants—a constant example —van Gogh represented many scenes with religious or philosophical overtones. *The Drinkers* by Daumier is such an image; in it the four ages of man are represented, all drinking around a table. The acerbic comment made by Daumier in his print is sharpened in van Gogh's painting. Its sonorous tones, completely different from those Daumier used in his paintings, caricature even more the figures of these men and the infant, who are literally drinking themselves to death.

Portrait of Madame Ginoux, 1890

Oil on canvas · 25½ × 19¼″ · Otterlo, Rijksmuseum Kröller-Müller

A FULLER, ALTOGETHER MORE ENTICING PORTRAIT of Madame Ginoux than the one executed at Arles (see *L'Arlésienne*), this picture is also a homage to Gauguin who had represented the sitter in the same attitude at the Night Cafe (Moscow, Pushkin Museum). Van Gogh executed four bust-length portraits of Madame Ginoux on differently colored backgrounds. He sent one to his friend and wrote him shortly afterward: ". . . it gives me enormous pleasure when you say the Arlésienne's portrait, which was based strictly on your drawing, is to your liking. I tried to be religiously faithful to your drawing, while nevertheless taking the liberty of interpreting through the medium of color the sober character and the style of the drawing in question. It is a synthesis of the Arlésiennes, if you like; as syntheses of the Arlésiennes are rare, take this as a work belonging to you and me as a summary of our months of work together. For my part I paid for doing it with another month of illness.''

The picture of this woman, with her enigmatic smile, represented for van Gogh the accomplishment of a dream: in the seclusion of the asylum, without Gauguin's presence but with the help of one of his drawings, he could finally achieve the full collaboration between two artists.

Vase with Irises, 1890

Oil on canvas · 36¼ × 29″ · Amsterdam, Rijksmuseum Vincent van Gogh

FLOWERS IN A VASE WERE A TRADITIONAL SUBJECT for van Gogh, as they had been earlier for the impressionists. In this canvas they are treated with a sureness of execution and a masterful bravura technique, which may reflect van Gogh's expectation of the new life awaiting him at Auvers. This canvas was one of the last done while at Saint-Rémy, and it was left behind to allow it time to dry. Another version—or rather, another view of the bouquet—was simultaneously painted against a pink background. Unlike the impressionists, van Gogh does not seek to represent the changing gradations of colors but, as in his portraits, strives for essential qualities whose intensity varies according to the colors of the backgrounds. Irises against pink are ''soft and harmonious,'' whereas in this version the yellow background and table create ''an effect of tremendously disparate complementaries, which strengthen each other by juxtaposition.'' Variations on two primary colors—blues going from pale to almost purple, and yellows going from light to ocher—give the picture an intricate diversity, which is cadenced by the powerful diagonals of their combinations: the green leaves of the flowers.

Portrait of Doctor Gachet, 1890

Oil on canvas · 26¾ × 22½" · Paris, Musée du Jeu de Paume

IN THE PERSON OF DR. GACHET, represented here in a meditative pose—evocative perhaps of the fact that he wrote his thesis on melancholia—van Gogh found a sympathetic character, responsive to his problems. Dr. Gachet had been recommended by Pissarro, whose works, along with other impressionist paintings, the doctor collected. Himself an amateur etcher, he was well disposed toward van Gogh; disconcerted at first by his work, he learned to like it. Van Gogh wrote about the pleasure the doctor eventually derived from looking at one of the portraits of Madame Ginoux (see *Portrait of Madame Ginoux*). Van Gogh's confidence in his new friend grew into identification: "I have found a true friend in Dr. Gachet, something like another brother, so much do we resemble each other physically and also mentally." For that reason, this portrait was conceived in the same spirit as the last self-portrait done at Saint-Rémy.

The formal arrangement of familiar objects—table, flowers—and the attitude of the sitter are similar to those in many portraits done at Arles. But the moving expression of the blue eyes, so clear and understanding, indicates a new psychological dimension. Van Gogh was, in fact, approaching a new type of modern portraiture. In "modern heads" (as opposed to ancient portraits) he found a "passion like a waiting for things, as well as a growth," and he added: "Sad and gentle, but clear and intelligent—this is how one ought to paint many portraits." The gentleness of the subject and his sweet disposition are expressed in a soft and undulating composition. The diagonal of the figure makes it appear more casual, less iconlike than the Arles portraits. Likewise, a subtle gradation of soothing blues replaces a strong background. Furthermore, van Gogh uses a broad and silky brushstroke, hardly broken to render the details of the face, which gives this portrait a rich, smooth texture.

Portrait of Marguerite Gachet at the Piano, 1890

Oil on canvas · 40⅛ × 19⅝″ · Basel, Kunstmuseum

THE BEAUTIFUL PORTRAIT OF MARGUERITE GACHET, the daughter of Dr. Gachet, at her music is unusual in van Gogh's oeuvre. The tall, narrow composition, the three-quarter view from the back, and the fact that the model is active are innovations, and van Gogh found them difficult to paint. Memories of impressionist compositions, Renoir's in particular, and of Toulouse-Lautrec's may to a certain extent account for this surprising image. The execution, however, is strictly van Gogh's and does not betray any concession to an impressionist technique. Particularly bold is the flat rendition of space: the wallpaper and rug are differentiated in texture, yet they form a coherent, decorative background for the figure. In this rare genre scene, van Gogh does not try, as in the portrait of Marguerite's father, to express profound feelings. Instead, the image has a pleasing and refreshing casualness enhanced by a variety of brushstrokes, which, as in earlier canvases, seem to change according to the surface van Gogh wants to represent: thick and swirling to follow the folds of the dress, thinned for the flat surface of the wallpaper, more textured for the rug, and broad and oily for the dark wood of the piano. Colors are also unusually delicate. Light pinks and pale lavenders are woven into the white texture of the dress with a delicacy that also recalls Toulouse-Lautrec. The same tones, only accentuated, are part of the wall and floor, with their complementary green.

Van Gogh thought increasingly of his paintings in terms of pendants, although no longer related in subject matter. He wrote about this canvas: "I have noticed that this canvas goes well with another horizontal one of wheat, as one is vertical and in pink tones, the other pale green and greenish-yellow, the complementary of pink; but we are still far from the time when people will understand the curious relation between one fragment of nature and another . . ."

Stairway at Auvers, 1890

Oil on canvas · 18⅞ × 27½″ · St. Louis Art Museum

THE WEEKS THAT PRECEDED VAN GOGH'S SUICIDE were marked by a considerable increase in production. In Auvers, close to Théo and supported by the understanding of such friends as Dr. Gachet, van Gogh rediscovered with satisfaction a countryside that provided him with suitable subjects. The little village had been visited by many Parisian artists: Monet and Renoir had painted there, as well as Pissarro and Cézanne. Although none of them were present during van Gogh's final days—only minor foreign painters were there—he could once again fantasize about the community of artists he had so much wanted to create. By being there, he belonged to a spiritual group whose activity was represented in the collection of Dr. Gachet. Auvers was not a revelation for van Gogh, as the South had been, but he found there a renewed interest in a northern, colder light, in houses that were not very different from those he had known in the Borinage. Furthermore, the lesson he had learned in Provence was by then so well assimilated that he could easily transpose it to different subjects.

Most of his landscapes done at Auvers, such as this street with a stairway, are joyful and richly organized canvases. This picture's composition is particularly close to that of the *Ravine* done at Saint-Rémy (see *Ravine of Les Peyroulets*). Bisecting diagonals, the attraction to a focal point immediately canceled by the busy, all-over activity of the entire canvas, even the pairing of little figures, recall that painting. But more than on a rigorous geometry, the picture relies upon a playful intricacy of arabesques and colors. The wavy movement of the stairs and of the grass creates an expressive design that is both structural and gratuitous: even the little patch of sky on the upper left corner is painted in coiling swirls, and such details as the scalloping ribbons over the yellow hats of the girls on the left are delightful to discover. Colors are distributed with the same freedom, in rapid, rhythmic movements—each tone echoed on both sides of the road, under the houses with the dominating red bar of their roofs.

Crows over the Wheatfield, 1890

Oil on canvas · 19⅞ × 39½″ · Amsterdam, Rijksmuseum Vincent van Gogh

WITH THIS PAINTING, EXECUTED IN THE FIELD where he shot himself a few days later, van Gogh brings his oeuvre to a poignant conclusion. "Sadness" and "extreme solitude" are words he used to express his mood while painting this work. He had recently visited his brother and sister-in-law in Paris. The visit had not been a successful one, and Vincent returned to Auvers, continuing to "feel the storm," and knowing that his life was "threatened at the very root" and that his "steps were also wavering." Brushes fell out of his hands as he was executing this picture, but habit and the overwhelming feelings he endured kept him going. The painting is unusually wide—a fact that accounts for its dramatic eloquence. Once again the opposition of earth and sky is essential to the meaning of the picture. In the lower tier, the animation of the wheat fields stirred up by an uncontrollable underground force undergoes a paroxysm. The horizon stops abruptly and the paths and movements of the wheat seem to converge toward the painter or the spectator, rather than to open up onto a wide perspective.

Although the painting transcends all interpretation, the inwardness of the composition reproduces the unbearable anguish of van Gogh's mind and his self-centered obsession. Van Gogh, who always favored simple color combinations, reduces them in this painting to an even barer and purer minimum; the black contours, that often underline his shapes do not exist in this painting. Black is limited to the hovering presence of the crows. The French poet Antonin Artaud said of this painting: "I hear the crows' wings beating like loudly clashing cymbals over an earth whose torrent van Gogh seems to have been no longer able to contain. And then death."

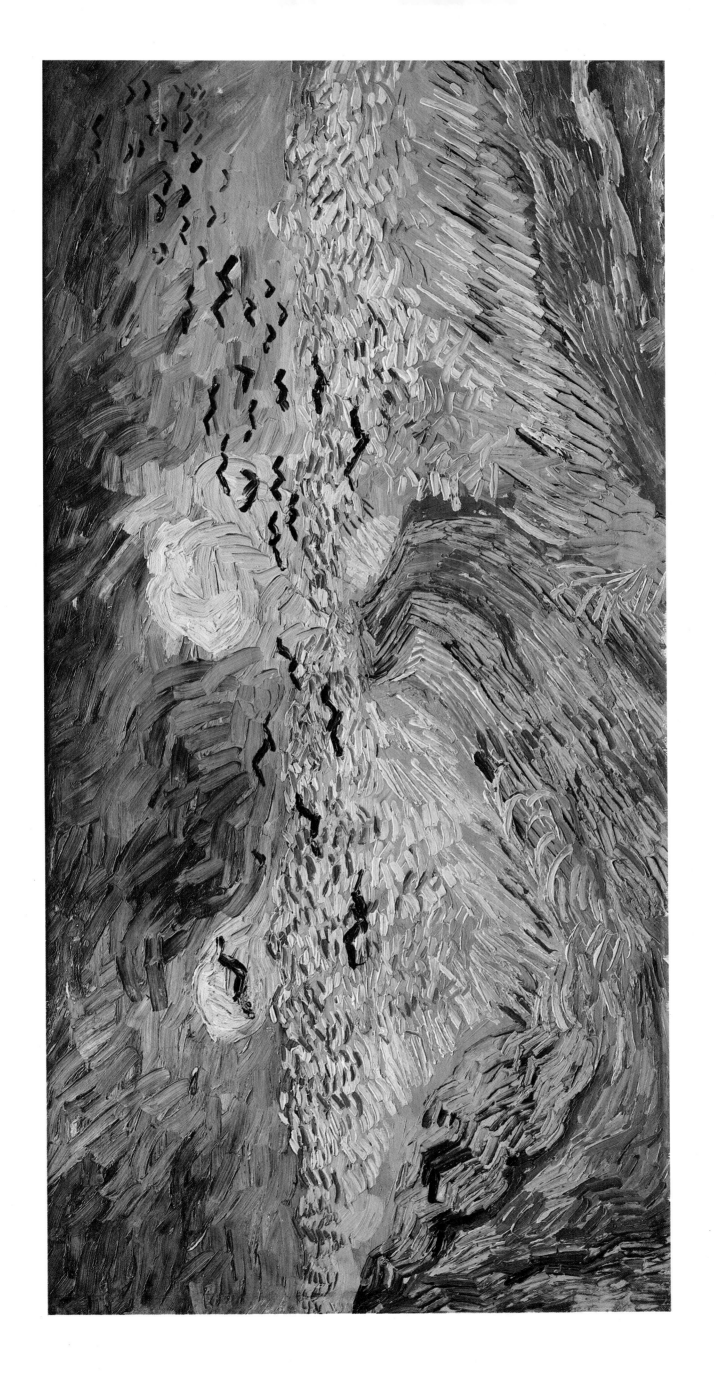

Self-Portrait with Bandaged Ear, 1889

Oil on canvas · 20 × 17¾″ · Athens, Stavros S. Niarchos Collection

THIS SELF-PORTRAIT WAS PAINTED IN JANUARY, 1889, at Arles while van Gogh was recuperating from his self-inflicted wound. Unique among van Gogh's portraits, its background is split by two colors, which cuts the composition into unequal parts at the level of the painter's eyes. It is an extraordinarily modern device, and knowing the importance van Gogh attached to the expressive meaning of the colors against which his portraits were set, one cannot help but think that it represents metaphorically his dual personality and his constant shifting between sanity and mental depression.

More haunting than other self-portraits, this masterpiece goes beyond the expression of fear and sadness, which is felt in the slightly opaque eyes and the movement of the lips. It is, above all, a great artist's self-portrait, which, like those of the aging Chardin, reveals— without spelling them out—personal contradictions and a disquieting inquisitiveness.

Flowering Almond Branch, 1890

Oil on canvas · 28¾ × 36¼″ · Amsterdam, Rijksmuseum Vincent van Gogh

THIS WONDERFULLY LIVELY PAINTING, one of the most Japanese works van Gogh ever executed, was done on a special occasion, the birth of Théo's son on January 31, 1890. Flowering blossoms had always represented for him a symbol of birth and juvenescense: upon arrival in Arles, he had painted a single blossoming twig in a glass of water to celebrate his new life. Van Gogh was very attached to this work and referred to it several times in his correspondence, announcing to his mother and sister the gift he was going to make to his brother. Shortly after he painted it, he suffered a strong attack of his illness and also wrote about it to his brother: "Work was going well, the last canvas of branches in bloom—you will see that it was perhaps what I have done most patiently and best, painted calmly and with a greater sureness of touch. And the next day, down and out like a beast."

Van Gogh's Bedroom at Arles, 1889

Oil on canvas · 28¾ × 36″ · The Art Institute of Chicago,
Helen Birch Bartlett Memorial Collection

AFTER AN ERRANT LIFE, A PLACE OF HIS OWN represented for van Gogh more than a shelter. The reports he sent to his brother on the progress he made on the house testify to his almost unhealthy obsession with it. The purchase of a bed, his plan to paint the room, the canvases he was going to hang on the wall especially in anticipation of Gauguin's arrival, were carefully described. He drew a view of this bedroom in a letter and eventually painted several versions of it in a style that he described as owing much to Seurat's simplicity. Van Gogh expressed above all the "solidity, stability and quiet" this bedroom gave him. He was proud of the way he had painted it, a "masculine workmanship, without stippling or hatching." It was also a reassuring image that he liked to contrast with the *Night Cafe*. Van Gogh felt the therapeutic effect of this soothing "still-life" during the convalescence after his self-inflicted mutilation: "When I saw my canvases after my illness," he wrote, "the one that seemed best to me was the bedroom."